I0776147

This book belongs to:

____

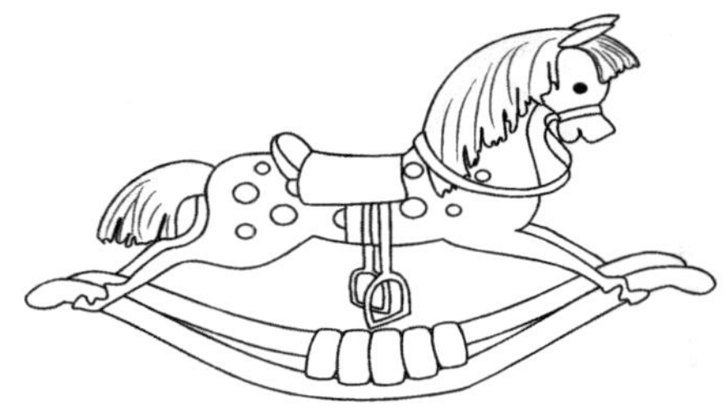

To A Very Sweet Godchild!
Merry Christmas
Coloring Card

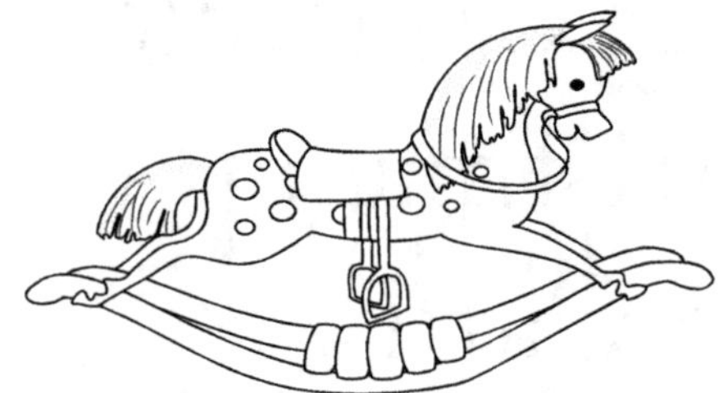

Joy to the world!

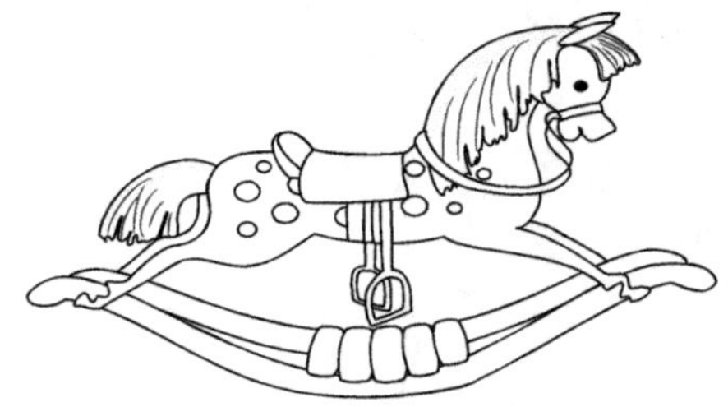

Warm wishes to you!

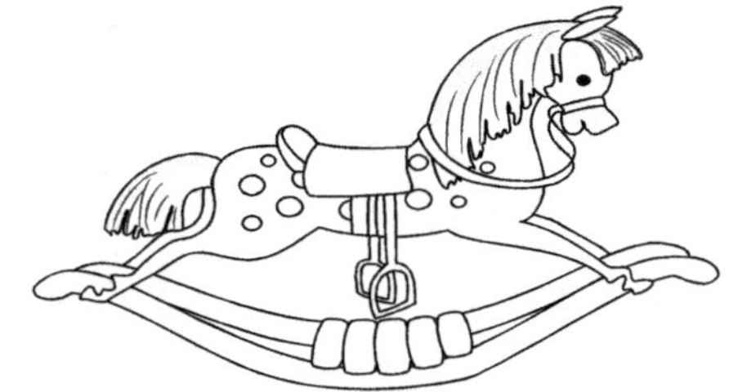

Merry and Bright!

Tis the season to be jolly,
fa la la la la la la la lamb!

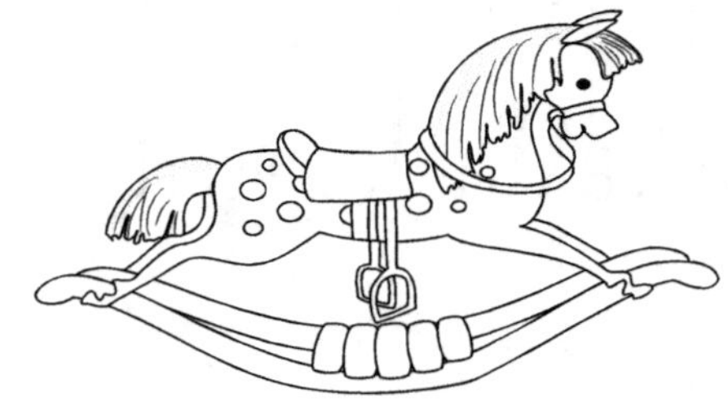

It's the best Christmas ever!

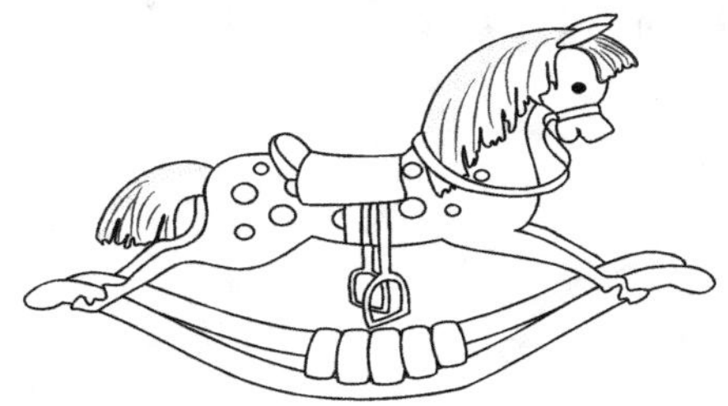

Joy to the animals!

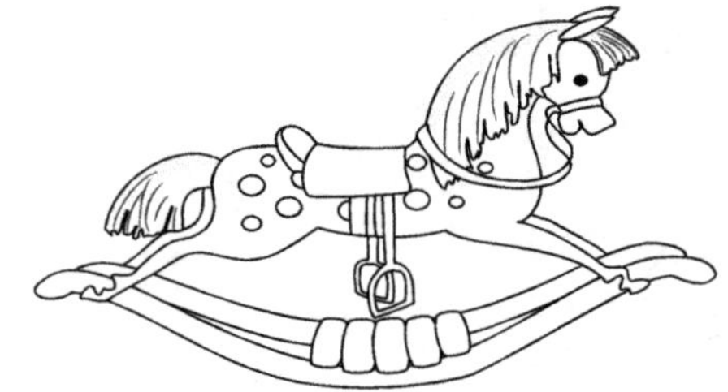

Santa's magic reindeer!

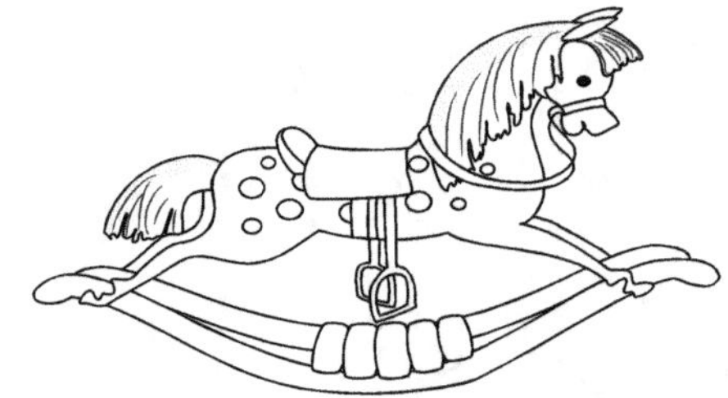

One of Santa's helpers!

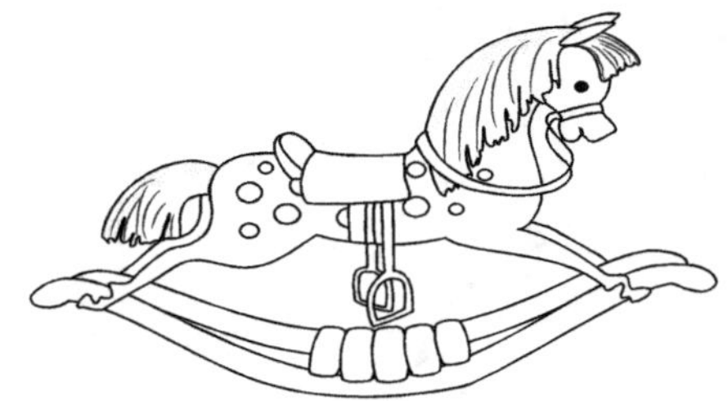

Flying in a winter wonderland!

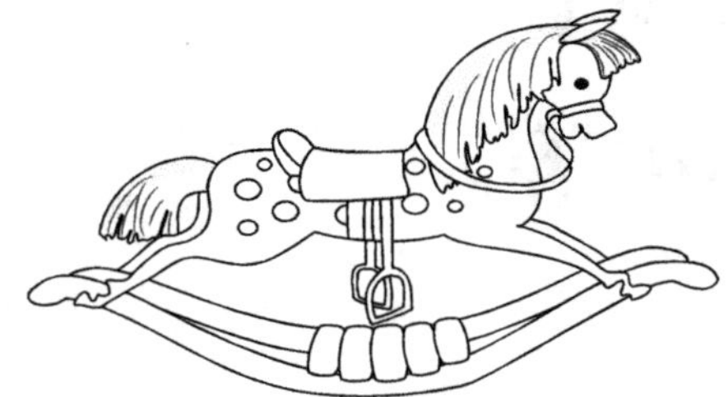

To A Very Sweet Godchild!
Merry Christmas
By Florabella Publishing, LLC

www.ingramcontent.com/pod-product-compliance
Lightning Source LLC
Chambersburg PA
CBHW060828260726
48660CB00003B/1146